The HOW-TO's of Life!
How to CALM DOWN!

featuring

Illustrated by Cecilia Coto

MEET THE CHARACTERS!

Sophie, a pink elephant, is very kind but extremely shy. She is often afraid of new situations and finds meeting new people difficult. Sophie is insecure about her unique, pink appearance.

Sparkelina®, a young girl, is the wisest of the group. She has spent many years observing children and is a patient and loving mentor to her friends Busybee and Sophie.

Busybee, a giant bee, is goodhearted, energetic, and impulsive. As a bee, he is used to flying freely from place to place and has a hard time understanding etiquette and rules.

Original Title: How to Calm Down!

Text: Kinderwise®
First Edition, March 2018

Illustrations: Cecilia Coto
Printed in U.S.A.

Copyright © 2017 by Kinderwise
ALL RIGHTS RESERVED.

ISBN 978-0-9987115-1-5

All rights reserved. No part of this publication, including but not limited to the content, illustrations, and names such as Sparkelina and Kinderwise may be reproduced, stored in a retrieval system, or transmitted in any form or by any means, electronic, mechanical, photocopying, recording or otherwise, without the prior written permission of the publisher. Unauthorized use or reproduction of any aspect of this publication is strictly prohibited and may result in legal action. For permissions, email creator and publisher at kinderwise@gmail.com.

BUSYBEE LEARNS HOW TO CALM DOWN!

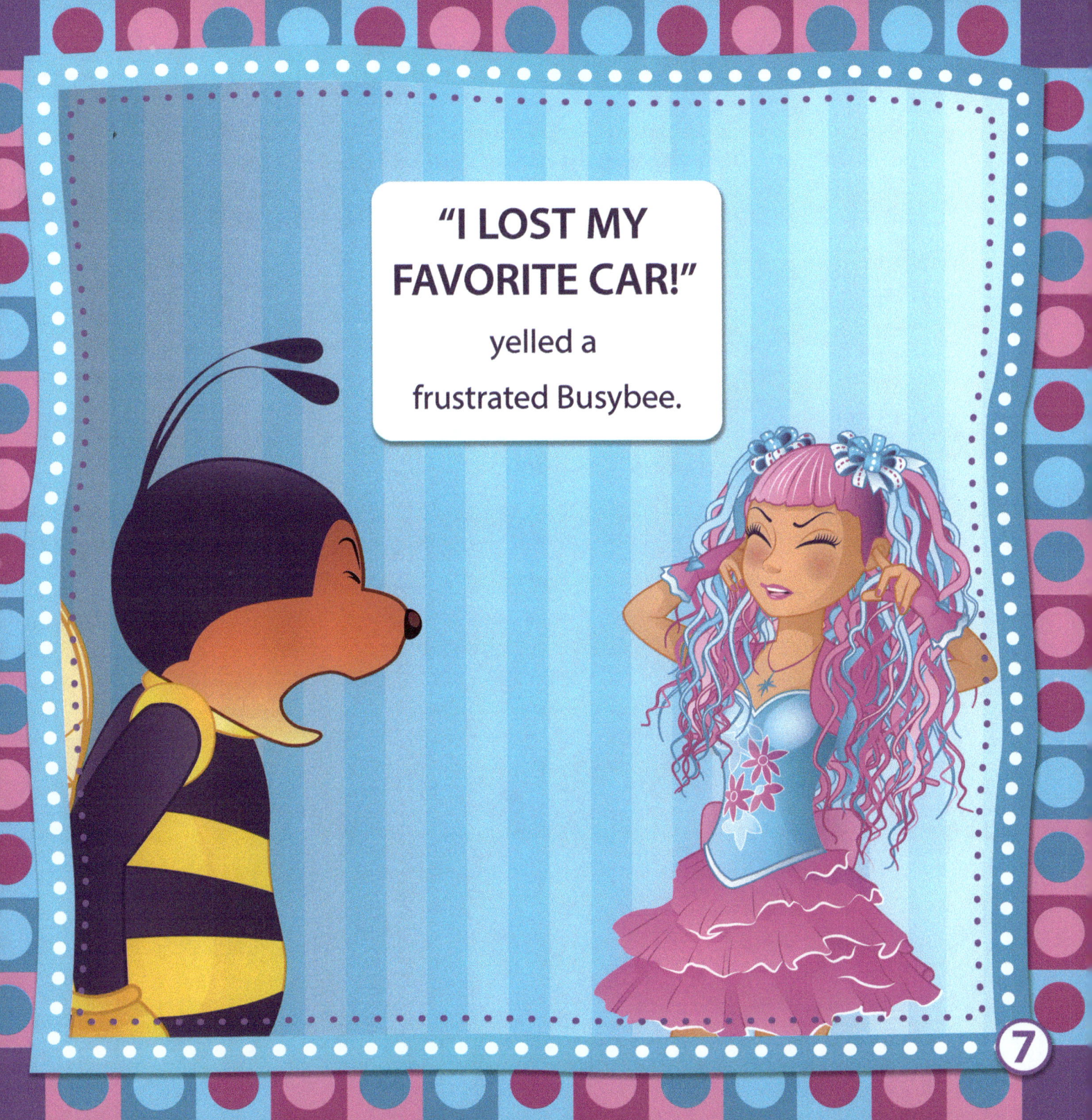

"**NOTHING!**" replied Busybee, remembering a lesson about patience he had learned a week earlier. "Busybee, I know a way to calm down," Sparkelina explained. "You can try it if you like."

STEP 1

"First, take in a deep, slow breath (as if you are smelling a flower). Make it last for a count of three." Busybee, trusting his friend, did what she said.

STEP 3

"Then, slowly blow at one finger (as if you're trying to blow out a candle). Think of something fun, like playing in the sand."

"Do this for all three fingers and each time as you blow out a candle curl down that finger. Repeat these three steps until you have blown out all three candles."

(BREATHE IN) STEP 1

(HOLD) STEP 2

(BREATHE OUT) STEP 3

"Do you feel better?" asked Sparkelina. "I do!" replied a relieved Busybee. "That's fantabulous. We can now go ahead and look for your car together," said Sparkelina.

"What does your car look like?" wondered Sparkelina. "Like a giant yellow and black bumble bee," Busybee answered.

"I was playing in my bedroom. It was right after I woke up this morning," Busybee recalled.

"Then I ate breakfast."

"Okay. We have searched both of those places and haven't found your car yet. Where else did you go?" asked Sparkelina.

Busybee and Sparkelina headed into Busybee's blue and white striped bathroom. They began to carefully explore.

Sparkelina opened up the medicine cabinet. Inside she saw Busybee's car gleaming in the light. "I fount it!" exclaimed Sparkelina.

Sparkelina smiled and said, "No problem, Busybee. I am happy to have helped out. That's what friends are for."

Busybee excitedly held his car up high in the air as he embraced her. He was proud to be friends with someone as patient, caring, and kind as Sparkelina.

A NOTE FROM SPARKELINA

WHEN YOU FEEL YOURSELF GETTING UPSET, TRY THIS BREATHING TECHNIQUE:

STEP 1:
BREATHE IN SLOWLY FOR A COUNT OF THREE AS IF YOU ARE SMELLING A FLOWER.

STEP 2:
AS YOU HOLD IN YOUR BREATH, HOLD UP THREE FINGERS. PRETEND THEY ARE CANDLES.

STEP 3:
SLOWLY BLOW AT ONE FINGER (AS IF YOU'RE TRYING TO BLOW OUT A CANDLE). THINK OF SOMETHING FUN. EACH TIME, AS YOU BLOW OUT A CANDLE, CURL DOWN THAT FINGER.

STEP 4:
REPEAT STEPS 1-3 UNTIL YOU HAVE BLOWN OUT ALL THREE CANDLES.

IT'S IMPORTANT TO LABEL YOUR EMOTIONS SO YOU CAN LEARN HOW TO BEST SOLVE THEM.

IF YOU'VE LOST SOMETHING, JUST RETRACE YOUR STEPS TO FIND YOUR MISSING ITEM.

AND, REMEMBER, WHAT DOES FUSSING GET YOU? NOTHING!

SOPHIE LEARNS HOW TO CALM DOWN!

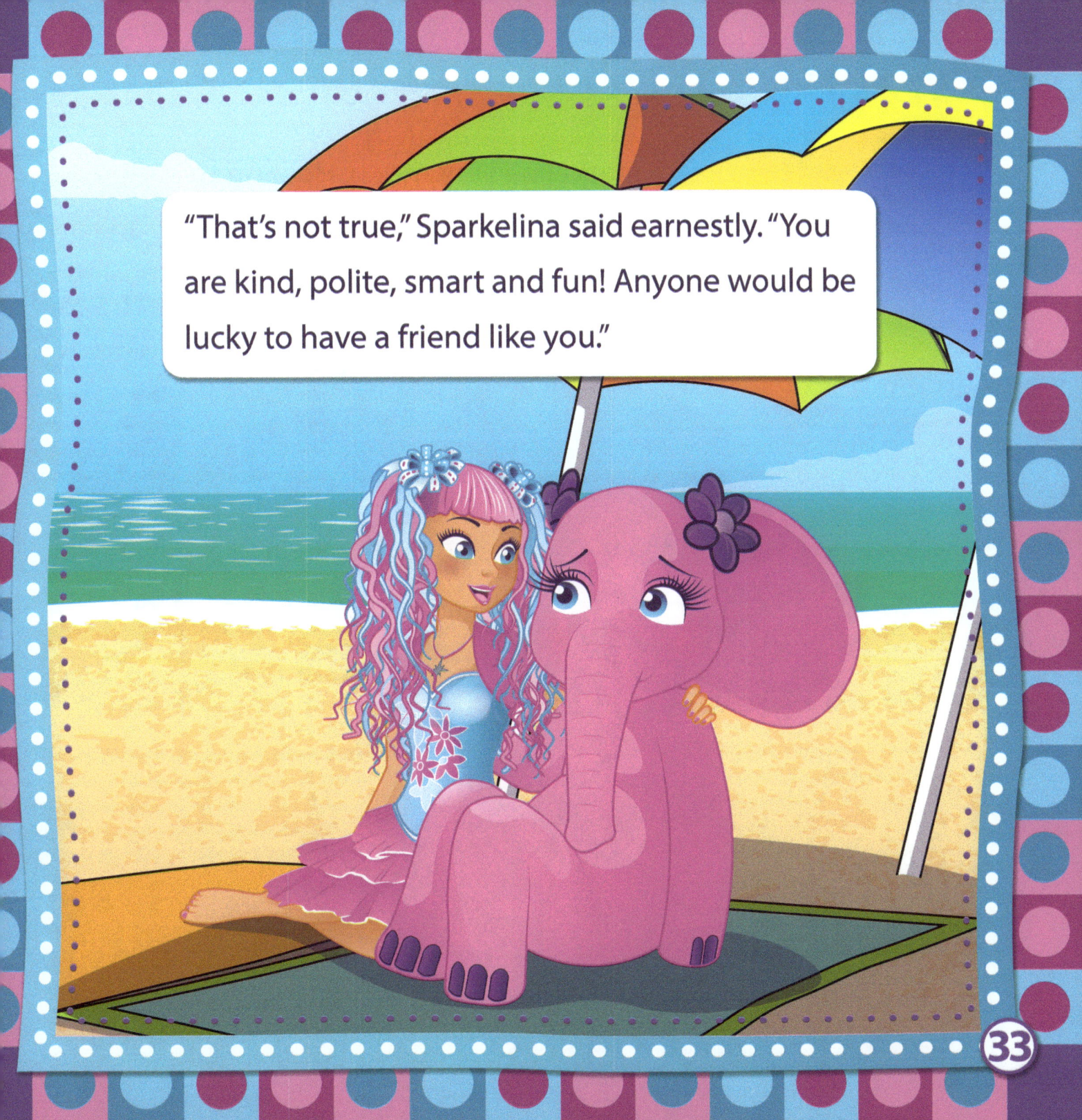

"That's not true," Sparkelina said earnestly. "You are kind, polite, smart and fun! Anyone would be lucky to have a friend like you."

Sophie trusted Sparkelina very much. Hearing this from her good friend made her feel better. "Thank you, Sparkelina," she said with a smile.

"Now, remember, if you aren't completely calmed down, you can always repeat Steps 1-3," Sparkelina explained.

1 2 3
(BREATHE IN)
STEP 1

1 2 3
(HOLD)
STEP 2

1 2 3
(BREATHE OUT)
STEP 3

Sparkelina noticed that Sophie did seem more confident now. She encouraged her to walk over to the grey elephant and ask him to play. That's just what Sophie did.

"Hi, I'm Sophie. Do you mind if I join you?" Sophie confidently asked the grey elephant. "I don't mind at all. My name is Gary. Grab a shovel and dig in, my friend," he said.

Sophie knew that she would not have found the courage to talk to Gary on her own. She looked back at Sparkelina and smiled.

Sparkelina smiled back and gave Sophie a thumbs-up. She was proud of Sophie. Sophie knew this and felt grateful to have a friend like Sparkelina.

A Note from Sparkelina

THE NEXT TIME YOU ARE FEELING STRESSED OUT OR NERVOUS, TRY THIS BREATHING TECHNIQUE:

STEP 1:
BREATHE IN SLOWLY FOR A COUNT OF THREE.

STEP 2:
HOLD IN YOUR BREATH FOR A COUNT OF THREE.

STEP 3:
SLOWLY BREATHE OUT FOR A COUNT OF THREE.

STEP 4:
REPEAT STEPS 1-3 AS NECESSARY.

ALWAYS REMEMBER THAT YOUR MIND IS VERY POWERFUL. TRY TO USE SELF-TALK WITH PHRASES LIKE "I CAN DO THIS," "I AM SMART," "I AM LIKEABLE," OR "I AM NICE."

POSITIVE SELF-TALK WILL HELP CALM YOU DOWN AND INCREASE YOUR SELF-ESTEEM.

ABOUT KINDERWISE®

Kinderwise® and characters were founded by a dedicated mother based in Southern California who recognized the importance of teaching children essential life skills in a memorable way. With a focus on emotional intelligence, she created an acclaimed book series entitled "Emotional Intelligence Program for Children" and other educational products "The HOW-TO's of LIFE" featuring her beloved characters Sparkelina® (a young girl), Busybee (a giant bee), and Sophie (a pink elephant). Together, these characters navigate the challenges of the world, learning valuable lessons in a delightful and engaging manner. Kinderwise® and characters aim to provide children with a fun and interactive learning experience, fostering personal growth and development.

Why an emotional intelligence book series? The desire for a clear, accessible approach to emotional intelligence development stemmed from the personal experience of the female founder of Kinderwise®. Raised by an orphaned mother with Asperger syndrome and a highly intelligent, yet anti-social father, she found childhood social interaction to be a challenge. She read book after book to "fill in the blanks" of her own lack of social knowledge. She discovered that empathy, awareness of feelings, self-regulation and people skills form the foundation for a successful, happy life.

This guide can be used to re-enforce the daily life lessons that the founder taught her own son. She felt it was important that the book be written from the perspective of a child. To do this, she created three imaginary friends. Much like children, these characters would have to learn how to get along with each other and others. *The How-To's of Life!* book series was born.

Your support helps Kinderwise® to continue creating educational books and products aimed at helping children develop essential social skills. For more information, email: kinderwise@gmail.com